# Consultant's Tool Box

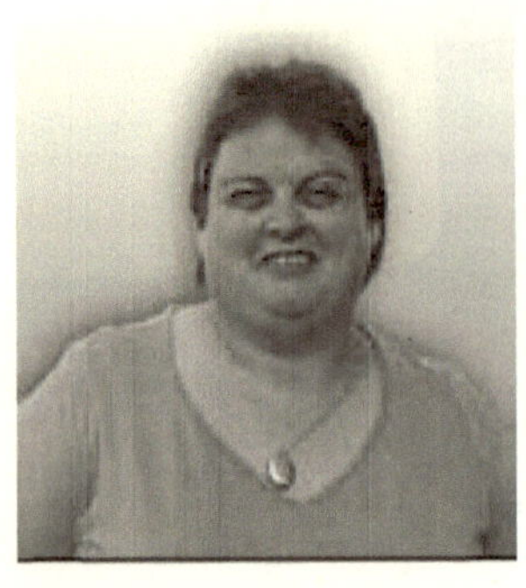

**Lee Lister** is a Business Consultant with more than 25 year's consultancy experience for many household names. On the internet she is known as The Bid Manager or The Biz Guru.

From an early age, she began an unparalleled journey through business consulting that continues to span across the UK, USA, Europe and Asia. She has consulted for many companies all over the world. Specialising in business change management, start up consultancy and trouble shooting. She is highly skilled in seminars, lectures and corporate presentations on business, project management and bid management. Lee's experience in marketing and internet marketing is also keenly sought after.

She is a prolific published writer of books, ebooks and articles on business, entrepreneurship and bid management. She can be found easily on major search engines and Amazon.

First published in Great Britain in 2010



**Publisher:** Biz Guru Ltd



**ISBN:** 978-0-9563861-4-4

# Consultant's Tool Box

*Methods, Procedures and Processes*

*That A Consultant Will Require*

**www.ProjectNiche.com**

This book is dedicated to my daughter Kerry Lister for whom I have always strived to be my best.

**Other books available include:**

FastTrack© Project Management

FastTrack© Bid Management

FastTrack© The Winning Solution

FastTrack© To Job Success

Proposal Writing For Smaller Businesses

## CONTENTS

## Your Tool Box

### Skills

## Activities

**Items**

## Legal Notice

**We do not believe in get rich quick schemes.** We do believe that success is equal parts of inspiration, hard work and luck. Every effort has been made to accurately represent our product and it's potential.

**Please remember** that each individual's success depends on his or her background, dedication, desire and motivation. As with any endeavour, there is an inherent risk of loss of capital. **There is no guarantee that you will earn any money**. This book will provide you with a number of suggestions you can use to better guarantee your chances for success. **We do not and cannot guarantee any level of profits.**

This product is written with the warning that any and every business venture contains risks, and any number of alternatives. We do not suggest that any one way is the right way or that our suggestions are the only way.

On the contrary, we advise that before investing any money in a venture you seek counselling and help from a qualified accountant and/or attorney or lawyer.

**You read and use this book on the strict understanding that you alone are responsible for the success or failure of your decisions relating to any information presented by our company Biz Guru Ltd.**

## Introduction

In the present climate, many people have considered becoming an independent consultant, lured by the flexibility and seemingly high financial gains. Other readers are internal consultants within a large company or are employed by a consultancy. This book seeks to answer most of your questions, remove the myths and give you a good understanding of what tools and skills a consultant should have in their Consultant's Toolbox. The key skills we want to help you with are:

- **Formal methods and processes** in order to define feasibility and produce cost benefits analysis and SWOT analysis.
- **Report writing** to produce the key tool of consulting - reports!
- **Presentations and meetings** to aid in gathering of requirements and presentation of results and reports.
- **Investigations**. Numerous different methods in order to formally collect and collate relevant facts and requirements.

## What Is Consulting?

Consulting is the offer, from one company to another, of fixed term, fixed rate work that is bound by contractual obligations, of the provision of expert skills or advice in exchange for monetary reward.

Consulting is very deliverable driven and the deliverables are frequently in the form of reports. A client is rarely going to pay you just to turn up and give a verbal recommendation with no reason to back up your proposals.

As the client is buying a service, it stands to reason that your skills and quality of deliverables should be high enough to warrant being paid for. Therefore, the first tools you need in your Consultant's box are skills and experience.

## Why are consultants used?

- **To provide expert advice** where that expertise may not be otherwise be available.

- **To collate enough information** to assist in a strategic decision. That is hiring the ability to gather requirements in an appropriate manner in sufficient depth to assist in strategic decision making.
- **To investigate the feasibility** of several options - again requirement gathering skills as well as the ability to propose and investigate several options.
- **To provide a separate, independent view** - independence coupled with experience and knowledge is required.
- **To be an "honest broker"** - the ability to see both sides as well as propose a solution that will meet the business requirement, but not necessarily the views of all.
- **To confirm a previous decision** - in this case, confirmation that a decision made is/was correct. Be careful of office politics here and ensure that you retain your integrity.

- **To manage at a senior level** - hiring senior management skills for an interim period.
- **To audit or quality review-** to audit or review deliverables, proposals, projects etc to meet quality standards. Sometimes to provide an independent opinion.
- **To provide expert labor** - hiring skill and experience at crucial times.
- **To cover for a shortage of staff** or to provide staff who are only needed for a short period such as a project.

## The Typical Consultant

A typical consultant must have all of the following personal attributes:

- **Self sufficiency** to work alone, find their own work, if necessary, and act upon their own skills and experience.
- **Confidence** to work with people at senior levels, to stand up in front of lots of strangers and talk about deep technical matters and start work in a company where you know no one.

- **Adaptability** to change so that you can cope with different company cultures, working practices, technical structures, software etc.
- **Marketing ability** in order to market your business and abilities.
- **Professionalism** in order to project professional personae.
- **Flexibility** in both working methods and living areas. Consultants frequently have to travel and stay away in order to complete a contract.
- **Drive.** Consulting can be difficult, especially when you are trying to get important concepts over to people who do not want to hear about difficult problems. When you are tired and frustrated with work, or desperate to find another contract, you have to have to put that smile on your face and keep going.

- **Organised**, just to keep your home and business together when you are living in a hotel for five nights a week, takes some organisation. Working in a strange company, often without a desk is difficult, and means that you always have to bring your own office with you. Lastly, working on a difficult consultancy assignment without a big company supporting you is difficult.

## Qualities Of A Good Consultant

- **Recognised experience and skill** - your client is buying your skills and experience after all.
- **Have good people communications skills** at all levels, especially at a senior level where your will be presenting your findings.
- **Able to quickly analyse a situation**. With consulting, speed of information assimilation is a key skill.

- **Can gather information effortlessly and painlessly.** You will need the right information in the right way.
- **Can provide detailed information and recommendations** in a collated and easily understood format.
- **Makes appropriate recommendations** and remains focussed on your terms of reference.

## Preparing For Consulting

Just as in any other business, your need to prepare yourself and your business environment so that you can work comfortably and effortlessly. Independent consulting is a career that involves a lot of tendering for work and travelling to the work you have won. Consulting within another company also involves you with extensive travelling, but often requires you to compete for the "good projects". Therefore, we will look at both getting work as well staying and working away.

## Your Services

Firstly, you need to look at your skills and experience and decide how you are going to market yourself and what services you are going to offer. In the IT world, this is easier because there are defined job structures and management levels as well as skills to slot yourself into.

Non-IT jobs are slightly harder to define and you should ideally seek out a niche that you can fill.

An example would be Lifestyle Guru, Home Organiser, Home Designer, etc. A niche is an area where you think that there is a need but there are few, if any, businesses meeting these needs. Niches, if you can find them are very fruitful.

One of the better ways to start is to have three of four services that you can offer. You can then build upon these offering bespoke services off of them as well as supporting products.

**Your CV/Resume**

An up to date CV or Resume will be the main tool of your trade. Make sure that yours is always current with your latest projects and customers and always to hand. It should have all the key skills requested mentioned on it.

Our book "*FastTrack To Job Success*" will help you with producing an interview winning CV or Resume. You can find it on Amazon or at www.JobSuccess.co.uk

You should also prepare a career summary – which is usually less than one page and is written in the third person. A good bio, again written in the third person, but much shorter could also be useful. Agencies and recruiters often ask for these and they are useful to put into your brochures and web site. Have a look at my bio at the front of the book for an idea of what they look like. Whilst we are on the subject, a great interviewing technique and an "interview suit" should be considered part of your Consultant's box.

## Your Rates

Once you have decided what services you are offering you need to set your rate. Obviously if you work for a larger company, they will do this for you. You do this by one or more of the following:

- Rates generally offered by the industry or by agents within the industry.
- Researching the market to find what other similar companies or services charge.

- What you believe the potential customers can afford.
- The rates the customer offers.
- Tendered project rates if you are part of a tender.

You should ensure that your rate would cover such costs as:

- Travel and subsistence to undertake the consultancy.
- Any resources you will need.
- Taxes and other legal expenses.

When setting your rates, ensure that the market will bear those rates - that is - will people pay them.

You should also ensure that you would have enough to live on when the non-paying periods arrive. The absolute maximum number of weeks that you will work will be 48 weeks - this takes out Christmas, Easter and public holidays.

It is more likely to be 42 weeks though because you will want a break, your might be ill and there will be short breaks between contracts. In reality, your maximum working time is more likely to be 25 – 30 weeks. This is because it can often take several weeks to find the next contract.

When working out the minimum I can charge, I usually take the daily rate minus £x for travel, hotel and subsistence. From this figure, I remove about 20% for tax and then multiply this final figure by 30 weeks or the number of weeks of the contract, if longer, and then decide whether I can pay my bills and my taxes for a year on this rate.

Different people and different types of consultancy will have different calculations but the above gives you an idea of what to include in your calculations.

## Marketing Pack

Now you have set your rates you need to set up your marketing pack. If you are working via agencies they will dictate what they require which is usually, CV/Resume, Career Summary and References. They may also require a sample of the type of projects or consultancy work you have undertaken recently. Sometimes lists of projects are requested.

Your CV should be of about 2 – 4 pages long with a summary of your skills and abilities at the top. Your career summary is about ½ page long and is a summary of your career to date written in the third party.

Your references should be from 2 -3 professional people and never given until asked for. This is because many agencies use them as marketing tools, contacting these peoples asking if they have any vacancies – this can really annoy your referees after a short while.

You should ensure that your control your CV/Resume. It is not unheard of them being used by unscrupulous agencies as they tender or tout for work. Of course, the resulting work does not necessarily come your way!

Similarly, CV's have been downloaded from job boards and used for less than legal means.

When an agency asks for your CV, ask about the job they are putting your forward to and request that it is only sent to a company after your have been informed and agreed. A reputable agency will agree to this, and it stops the embarrassment of two or more agencies sending your CV to the same company – or worse still the company you work for now!

If you are not working via agencies, your marketing pack will be slightly different. You should design and print some quality brochures, which display your details, photo and services. Your prices should not be displayed as this gives you some negotiation and flexibility.

A business card and web site are also very important as they project your professional image.

You should also set up a good filing system and contact database to hold details of your clients and the work that your have undertaken for them. Your database is also a good marketing tool, enabling you to market further services to them, or request references or referrals from them.

All of your documentation should be standardised and of good quality. A good logo and some branding makes your company look very professional.

When meeting clients and working on site you should be dressed very professionally as well as carrying a good quality briefcase or bag.

## Your Mobile Office

You will also need to set up a mobile office. You will need a laptop, telephone, email and access to your web site. This can be solved with a quality laptop, mobile phone and wi-fi access to your email account. A web site can easily be set up via a provider such as Godaddy or Hostgator or you can design your own if you feel you have the skills.

Well first start with your laptop – make it as light and as powerful as you can afford. I say light, because anything that weighs more than 5lb is going to be one laptop that you really hate after you have hauled it around for a few hours. Some models have CD/DVD units that plug in to the main PC. These are useful if you leave them behind or pack them separately. I prefer them to be included if possible. A small mouse and slim mouse pad – the latter which stores inside the "clam" of the laptop when travelling to protect the screen – completes your basic office.

I also have a handful of those memory sticks that plug into your USB socket. These hold my key documents and any documents that I am working on now. In that way, if I cannot find a broadband link to hop onto when travelling, I can at least use the local internet café and still have my documents available. It is always a good idea, to set up a web mail account, and use your own email settings, as a fall back. Lastly, I always carry a couple of CD's with all my documents and emails on – just in case the awful happens and my laptop ceases working or is stolen.

I solve the telephone problem by having a VOIP phone number for the major areas that I work in, which can be transferred to my mobile phone at little cost. Other people transfer their office/home phone to their mobile phone. Yet others have a "0800" number, or similar, and have this directed to whatever phone they are near at any given time. Mobile phones can also be used to download your emails and many mobile phone providers offer mobile based internet access.

A quality leather folio or folder to hold your papers, calculator and business cards always looks professional when talking to your clients. I also have pens, pencils a ruler, clips and a stapler in a quality (no fluffy or Disney characters) pencil case. Thanks to technology, I can now get my travelling office into a briefcase and am well versed in working in hotels, restaurants, cars and coffee shops as well as car parks sometimes.

To carry my laptop, well aware that passing through numerous security checks with the laptop out of the bag, as well as a higher risk of it being stolen. I actually carry my laptop inside a case logic slip case – inside of my rolling bag. In this way, it is hidden from view, but easy to get to when going through security checks. For general use, I have another case logic carrier that hangs off my shoulder. For the less secure areas, and if I have to store the laptop in the hotel room, I have a "safe" which is a mesh bag attached to a long lead that can be wrapped around something solid and then locked.

The bag and the lead cannot be cut. These can be found at good camping shops. Of course, my laptop is password protected and can be attached to the desk by a lead if necessary.

A mobile/cell phone, a broadband dongle, small headphone/microphone and small digital camera completes my office and a MP3 player my working environment.

So that is my office, but of course, I am dependant upon broadband for it to work. Luckily, wi fi areas are easier to find now – let's just say I drink a lot of coffee. Places like Starbucks and McDonalds, hotels, airports etc. You get to know the possible areas very quickly, you can seek them out beforehand using the internet, or buy a small wi fi hotspots seeking gizmo. I have always found these places welcoming, if you sit down, buy their products and do not cause any disruption. I usually ask if I can plug in as well.

The only problem I find, apart from too much caffeine, is when you need to use the facilities – in this case, knowing that my laptop can run faster than I can, it comes in with me. More of a problem for the gents I think.

Of course, the availability of broadband dongles now means that you can theoretically work anywhere – but the speeds are not always faster enough for a decent workload!

## Staying Away

Your work will often involve staying away which is not only hard work for you, but hard on your luggage as well. Buy good quality, professional looking luggage and keep as much of it ready packed as possible. Unpacking and packing soon gets very annoying when done for three months at a time - far better to just pick up a bag, throw a few clothes in and go off. As well as the normal things, you should include an extension lead, as sockets are never where you want them to be!

To help with your accounting, it is better to make payments on just one credit card and keep all receipts. Your accountant will advise on the types and levels of expenses that will be appropriate. If you work for a company, they will often pay for the hotel and you pick up the extras, which your company will want to see receipts for.

I have a small plastic zip file that holds all my receipts and I just empty it out each month. Lastly, do not forget to keep in touch with the loved ones at home!

## The Important People in your Life

Just as you need things in your life in order to make your life go smoothly, so you need some very important people. These are:

- Your accountant.
- Your partner.
- Your agent(s).

## Your Accountant

Whilst you will not need an accountant if you work for a large company, independents certainly will – if only to pay the least possible tax. What can they do for you for you?

- Set up your company.
- Advise on expenses, dividends, salaries etc
- Prepare and audit your accounts.
- Prepare your VAT, salary returns etc.
- Prepare your taxation returns.
- Prepare your personal tax returns.

The recommendation is that you allow your accountant to do as much work as you can reasonable afford. Taxation for directors is quite complex, as is the type of expenses that you can claim. In some countries, your company accounts will need to be audited by an accountant before filing.

It is advisable to have an accountant that understands the needs of a consultant and a one director company. This is very important because of the peculiarities of the expenses and company set-up. Consultants are one of the groups of companies that the Inland Revenue (UK) takes particular interest in and some taxation laws have been passed that are aimed at mainly this group.

**Your Partner**

If you have a personal or business partner, they need to have a special understanding about your way of life. You will often be working away and be without income.

Here are some good things that come out of having a supportive partner.

- **Company Secretary.** Companies require a Company Secretary, separate from the Managing Director, who is responsible for signing off dividends etc. A trusted partner is appropriate for this position. In some countries and cases this is no longer required - check with your accountant.
- **Profit sharing.** By becoming a shareholder, dividends can be paid out of the company directly to the partner. This is tax advantage when your own income is nearing the next tax bracket and your partner has a lesser income. Your accountant will advise.
- **Supporting income.** In those difficult times, it takes the pressure off of you and allows you to be more choosy about your next contract or assignment.
- **Company administration.** Two people working on this, as well as another person to answer the phone, takes away some of these burdens.

- **Agency contact.** The world of consulting means that agencies always want you to be readily available; otherwise they go onto the next person on the list. Having a second person available to answer the phone is great!

## Your Agent

Most computing consultants go through an agency for the following reasons:

- They have many company contacts so that they can more easily find your next contract.
- They act as a go-between you and the prospective company's HR group so that they can promote your strengths and they do much of the paperwork.
- Many large companies now have Preferred Supplier lists that you will probably not be on but the agent will be.
- They sets-up the interviews and deal with all these details.

- They pay your company at the end of the week or month, often before they are paid. This smoothes your cash flow and lets you know when you will be receiving your cash - often straight into your company bank account.

For this work, they take a percentage cut of 10-25% of any contract. This may seem a lot, but the ability to find contracts and smooth out your cash flow is well worth this discount.

If you find an agency who wants to charge less than 10% you should be wary that they are around to make your payment when due. The company you consult with only has a contract with the agent - not you. It is not unheard of for an agency to go bust, leaving their contractors unpaid and unable to do anything about it.

A reputable agent will not charge for finding you a contract - they only charge a mark-up. Anything else if probably a scam.

## Your Relationship with your Agent

Many large companies have preferred supplier agreements with approx. 1-6 agencies, which tend to be the larger agencies. If you wish to work for X company then only a preferred supplier can put you forward, although some small agencies can circumnavigate this. A large agency has contacts with many large companies and is on a number of preferred supplier lists. A smaller agency usually has a more personal contact with their clients and has to try harder.

Consultants are a very mobile breed so tend to be registered with a number of different agencies. Agents know and understand this so do not be embarrassed about it. Your relationship should be:

Professional **– which we all are.**

- **Friendly** - we all like to enjoy our work and making your agent feel welcome is a good way to ensure that they keep ringing back.

- **Keep up contact** so that you do not fall to the bottom of the pile. Do not harass them either. Agents generally only get paid on results so if they have something for you, they will ring!
- **Database skill search.** They use a database to identify consultants with the skills and experience that the customer has asked for. So set your C.V. up so that they can easily find you.

**They choose a few from many.** Most companies now only allow agencies to send a small specific number of CV's to them. After a brief screening chat with you, they will either put you on the list or tell you that you are not suitable. Just remember how important this chat can be – so always be "on message", friendly and available.

## Charge Out Rates

Probably nothing generates more confusion, distrust and envy than the matter of charge out rates. Usually the client believes either that the consultancy is making an abnormally high profit from the use of contractual staff, or the users believe that the consultant is in receipt of this abnormally high remuneration. This is definitely one piece of information best kept from both your staff and your users.

Care must be taken to ensure that the charge out rates for your staff accurately reflect the costs of undertaking the work, but also great care must be taken to ensure that the clients are aware precisely what they are going to receive for their expenditure.

Charge out rates are usually the only method of the consultancy receiving payment for work done. Most pre-contract work is undertaken speculatively and at no cost to the client.

This "free time" must also be computed into the equation.

As a rough guide, 50 % of the costs should appertain to the remuneration package. Many large companies have charge out rates of 2 - 3 times the team member's remuneration. This is acceptable and is due to the heavy overheads of large company and the costs of the support functions that allow the project to be gained and funded.

Fixed price contracts are even more difficult to calculate. You start by carefully estimating how long the contract will take and how many staff you need. It is also better to add a 10% contingency to this calculation.

The charge out rate for a member of the project team should be calculated as follows.

Remuneration of team member

\+

Benefit package of team member

\+

Costs of finding team member

\+

Administration costs of employing team member

\+

Costs of training and keeping team member

\+

Project administration overheads

\+

Profit

---

CHARGE OUT RATE

---

Due care should be taken to ensure opportunity costs - the income lost from not pursuing other activities, are also computed within the equation.

## Writing A Winning Proposal?

You've been working with a potential client and you think that you finally have the future project all worked out - then they ask you for a proposal. You have seen this great potential project but you need to bid for it. So how do you write that proposal that is going to win you the business?

Well first let us look at what the proposal should do. Win of course, but before that you have to:

- Make your company stand out from the others as well as reflect the values and brand of your company.
- Offer the solution that is required in a format that is easily understood.
- Be well priced so as to attract the client, provide a profit for your company as well as opportunities for you both to work together in the future.
- Be well structured, well written and well presented.

Bearing in mind the above, your proposal should look something like this:

1) Thanks for the opportunity.

2) Your understanding of the job that needs to be done.

3) How you would complete the job, how long it will take and who will do it.

4) Why your company is the best for the job.

5) Your price - with subject breakdowns if appropriate.

6) Any "must haves" assumptions made etc in getting to the price.

7) Last thanks and way forward.

Item 5 and 6 should be on their own page so that they can be removed if necessary.

Remember to put your company details and contact details on the header of each page and your copyrights, date and page number of number of pages on each footer.

When you send off the proposal, on time of course, include a brief cover letter, with:

- Your contact details.
- The name of the person who is their contact for this bid.
- Your thanks for the opportunity.
- A very brief overview of bid - no price.
- A period that bid is current.
- Your thanks and hope to hear from them soon.

Now sit back and pride yourself on a job well done. Good luck

## The Art of Selling

It has been said that a sale is really closed long before the seller makes the final pitch to the customer. In many ways, this is very true. Many customers make a decision to buy in five minutes or less of being introduced to the product. As a successful entrepreneur, it is up to you to make those five minutes really count.

There are a couple of important things that take place in this five minute window of opportunity.

First, the customer decides whether or not it is worth the time to learn more about the product. If the answer is no, then even thirty minutes of a great pitch will accomplish nothing.

Second, the customer will think of major obstacles that will prevent the purchase from taking place. If a customer decides the product is out of reach for some reason, that will make everything that follows that first five minutes of no value whatsoever.

Your job is to overcome both these issues and encourage the prospect to not only desire the product, but also be able to visualise actively using the product to great advantage. Here are a few ideas on how to accomplish this:

- **Ascertain the needs of your client.** This means asking clarifying questions that help to narrow the focus of the presentation to what is important to the customer. For example, if a primary need of the client is to pay the phone bill at the end of the month, tailor the presentation to show how the product can directly help achieve that goal.
- **Be prepared to address common obstacles.** Many obstacles are not unique - people from all sorts of background will share the same concerns. Proactively bring those up during those first five minutes and quickly demonstrate how they are non-issues. This will make it possible to dispose of those concerns and hold the attention and interest of the prospect past that five minute window.

- **Always close with benefits**. Some of those benefits may have to do with overcoming obstacles, but go a little further than that. Using the phone bill example again, point out how the product can make it easier every month to pay the bill not just the one that is due the end of this month.

Making the most of those first five minutes will greatly increase your chances of closing the sale. Spend some time working on a model presentation and critique the results.

## Working With Your Client

The Client Relationship is possibly the most important relationship within the project that you can have. It involves holding regular meetings with clients to understand:

- The client's business.
- What they want to achieve from the consultancy.
- What their constraints and business risks are.

When talking to senior users or project sponsors a good client relationship helps you to garner information. It makes the definition of the Business Requirements and the Scope and Objectives, rapid and fairly painless.

Client relationship is a two way matter they will also expect you to analyse the mass of information about the client's business and provide regular updates on progress, problems and issues that need resolving.

They will want you to provide a non biased view and suggest a varied range of detailed options as to what can be achieved. To build the client relationship, you should:

- **Build rapport and mutual understanding.** You both have to work together for some time in order to produce something of value. You should support each other regardless of internal politics, consultancy problems etc.
- **Build trust and cooperation** and ensure that you understand their business problems.
- **Analyse the information given to you.** During the project, you will be bombarded by information from all areas, some of it conflicting. The skill of the consultant is in understanding which information to work with and which to discard.
- **Tactfully request any other information required**. Know how to ask for that elusive piece of information!
- **Provide an alternative way of looking at matters**. When people get very close to

a problem they can be focussed on certain aspects. It is sometimes refreshing to hear another viewpoint. TACTFULLY.

- **Recommend alternative solutions**. Your client is probably expecting more than one answer to their problems so that they can make informed decisions.
- **Motivate the production of information** and progress to your stated closing point.
- **Ensure that the client gains from the relationship.** Your client will usually welcome the chance to learn from the experience – it stops boredom and enhances their reputation and career prospects. Make sure that you facilitate this and you will probably learn as well.

**Golden Rule** – those that sign the cheque have the final say!!

## Scoping and Defining Objectives

Before you dive into a consulting assignment, you need to define the scope and objectives of your consultancy.

### The Scope

This is the boundary of what you will looking at. It is important to set your scope because:

- It defines your assignment
- It maintains your focus
- It saves time and money
- It clarifies matters

No activity is an island or can stand alone. You also need to define the boundaries and handoffs to other areas, groups and processes.

By defining the boundaries, everyone is clear on what and where you will be working. By defining the handoffs, others are aware as to where their responsibilities start and end.

## The Objectives

These are what you are trying to achieve. It is usual to have 3 – 5 objectives which

- Define your assignment.
- Maintain your focus.
- Provide measurable goals.
- Define your deliverables from the assignment.

Your scope and objectives will consist of:

- The business requirement that needs to be solved.
- Any business problems that exists.
- Any restrictions, business, resource or technological based.
- How you will be measured and what will be measured.
- The deliverables you are expected to produce.

## The Business Requirement

The Business Requirement seeks to address business problems, changes and wishes e.g.

- Changes company strategy or direction.
- The business issues not being met.
- Problems caused by the technical platform.
- Changes in organisational structure.
- Changes in the business market.

Typical changes and problems are:

- Changes in the company strategy.
- Business issues not being met.
- Problems caused by the technical platform.
- Changes in organisational structure.
- Changes in the business market.

Typical risks would be:

- Loss of market share or brand strength.
- Adverse profit changes.
- Unable to support the new environment.
- Loss of key staff.
- Problems in product fulfilment.

Typical constraints would be:

- Money.
- Time.
- Technical environment.
- Market forces.
- Skills availability.
- Solution availability.

When reviewing the Business Requirement and options, plan your approach by considering these events:

- **Organisation** – is it going to change? Must it change to address the Business Requirement?
- **Business** – market forces, aims of the business etc.
- **User** – nature of the users, skill level, adaptability etc.
- **System** – constraints, upgrade path, costs.
- **Resources** – availability, marginal costs.
- **Constraints and problems** – what are they and what are their effects?
- **Advantages** – what does your client get out it in exchange for cost and upheaval?

The decision as to what option to follow will be made by weighing: Costs, Upheaval, Time, Results, Resource Availability and Problems Overcome against the Perceived Value of the end product i.e.

**Benefits > Costs + Changes Made**

The Business Requirement can be the single most important task that a Consultant is charged with.

**Remember:** Without a clear and agreed definition of the Business Requirement, any project will quickly lose direction and not meet the needs of the users.

The Business Requirement must be:

- Clearly defined
- Formally agreed by the sponsor
- Totally nailed down

**Always, Always**

Define the actual Problem and its Requirements

Not their idea of what it is!

To ensure this, you must go out and gather enough data to be able to make an informed proposal. You need to investigate the:

- Organisation.
- Business.
- User.
- System.
- Resources.
- Constraints and problems.
- Advantages.

**From problem to proposal**

- Define the business requirement.
- Ascertain the objectives and constraints.
- Define the problem.
- Gather the user requirements.
- Ascertain options.
- Define proposals.
- Document and present.

Just remember - what does the client want?

They have a business problem or business requirement and do not know what solution is available or sometimes what they want. After all that is why he is hiring a Consultant!

Do not forget you are the solution to the problem – Not part of it!!!

Your principle responsibility is to end your assignment with a delighted client and a very happy (and still sane) consultant.

**Refining A Requirements During A Project**

We need to consider:

- What the requirement is? – Not as easy as it sounds! The requirement gets muddled up with the desire for new technology, what the sales agent said, a desire to meet the challenge of a new competitor etc.
- What the possible solutions are?
- How to get from one to another.

## Definition of A Business Requirement

The Business Requirement is what the **business** requires to do one or more of the following:

- Meet a change in the business environment.
- Meet a business challenge - e.g. increase competitiveness.
- Respond to a marketing challenge - e.g. increase brand awareness.
- Grow or contract the business - e.g. merger.
- Respond to technical or technological obsolesce (or threat of) - e.g. Year 2000.
- Respond to a Force Majeure - e.g. fire
- Save labor or other resource costs - e.g. consolidation.
- Improve customer service - e.g. provision of call centre.
- Improve the collection, collation control and/or dispersion of information - e.g. data warehouse.

- To allow an organisation to make innovative or unique changes or strides within their environment – e.g. electronic commerce (loyalty cards was an example).

**From Problem to Proposal**

- Define the Business Requirement – What, Why, When.
- Ascertain the Objectives and Constraints – e.g. budget, time, quality, brand image, market, and product.
- Define the Problem – Why Not?
- Gather the User Requirements – What, Why, How, When.
- Ascertain Options – always include "do-nothing" option.
- Define Proposals – give proposal for each option.
- Document and Present – formally document in a logical and effective way.

Consider the following scenarios for Options/Proposals:

- The best option possible if one or more of the constraints was not there - sets "ball park" - particularly useful if one or more of the constraints seriously affects the options.
- The best option if all constraints were operational.
- Other options possible, working under some of the constraints.
- The best option solution to the problem.
- The do-nothing scenario.

It is usual to rank the Options/Proposals either by most expensive first or by the most appropriate first.

The skill of the consultant is to:

- Define the business requirement.
- Ascertain any restrictions, business, resource or technological based.
- Ascertain any business problems.
- Visualise possible solutions.
- Define and present the proposed solution.
- Inspire, motivate and calm any fears.

The best way to structure my analysis of business requirements is to section the analysis into:

- Business.
- Users.
- System.
- Organisational.
- Resources.
- Constraints and Problems.
- Advantages.

## Requirement Gathering

There is no doubt that the largest job a consultant will undertake is requirement gathering. There are numerous ways that this can be undertaken and the most popular are:

- Interviews with the client.
- Interviews with the users.
- Meetings.
- Questionnaires.
- "Walk throughs" and Process Mapping
- Workshops.
- Prototyping.

In order to obtain requirements, you will need to gather a great deal of data, which should be:

- Structured.
- Documented.
- Communicated.
- Controlled.
- Pertinent.
- Efficient.
- Inoffensive.

How much data do you need to gather depends what you are going to do with it:

**Options and Proposals:** Obviously, you need to be quite detailed in your requirement gathering if you are going to make proposals on how a business is to move forward. Similarly, as you are reviewing several options, you will need to look at the requirements in several different ways in order to investigate sufficient options to make viable proposals.

## An Interview With Your Client

This is one of the most important tasks you will have. Not only will you have an opportunity to obtain information "straight from the horse's mouth", but you will also be able to establish your credentials and status on the project. Obviously, the latter should be done subtly and effortlessly.

You should prepare for these meetings and send, in good time, your client a list of matters that you wish to discuss. This allows them time to prepare the information that you will need and gives them a sense of security. You should also give them an idea of the possible length of the meeting and keep to it. Your client will be busy and appreciate this and it is their choice as to whether they wish to extend this time.

If find the best way to manage these kinds of meetings is to have a tick list of questions that you wish to ask, but ask them in a conversational way.

This method allows you to wander a little in your discussions and maybe bring up other items. Do not be afraid to let your client discuss matters outside of the remit, but also do not be afraid to politely bring your client back on subject every so often. Remember to capture the essence of why you are being employed on this consulting activity and what they are aiming to achieve.

**Suggested Client Interview Format**

1. Introduction and aim of interview
2. Subject area 1 then its summary.
3. Subject area 2 then its summary.
4. Subject area 3 then its summary. Ideally, this is all the subjects that should be covered.
5. Summary of items covered.
6. Conclusion and way forward.

## Questions To Ask Your Client

There are a number of questions that must be asked when interviewing your client.

It does not matter what project you are going to undertake. It is not important what industry you are going to be assessing. What is important is you know what you are going to do and what the client wants. Here is a list of the obvious questions every good consultant should know the answer to *before* starting a project.

1. **What business problem are you hoping to solve by developing this project?** If you do not understand what the problem is then you cannot help to solve it. Sometimes it may not be clear as to what the client actually wants. The scope may only tell you what they would like to see happen. You need to be focused on what the true issues are so that you can solve business needs not business wishes.

2. **What is the business currently doing to alleviate or solve the issue?** You must understand what the client is doing in order to understand what must be done. You do not want to develop a project plan overview only to have someone tell you it has been tried. Find out what they have done. Ask questions while you are listening. You should particularly listen to what has not worked and why it did not work. In this way, you do not duplicate work.

3. **What internal resources will this project be utilising?** What outside resources will be necessary? You will want to determine where your help and team players are coming from. You may be familiar with most of the company, but if the client wants to outsource some activities. it may become more of a problem. You may have to make a list of external interactions. You need to understand your commitments on the project.

4. **Do you have a vision for the project?** The best projects work towards a business vision. You need to understand the end requirements and how to meet it.

5. **What risks to you foresee and are you willing to take them?** A conservative client may not be inclined to take large risks. Getting them to be specific can help when generating the consultancy program. You may also be able to overcome some of their fears or doubts by explaining the risk factor more thoroughly.

6. **Are you under any type of time constraint?** Most clients have time constraints which affect every avenue of business. You will want to know what these are and plan accordingly.

7. **What is the projected budget and can it be deviated from?** It is important when planning your project, that you understand the budgets and resources available so that you can choose the most efficient approach. There are times when a project may run over budget and you need to know your leeway.

8. **Who is the end user?** Who are you working for and who is in charge? What support will they have? You will need to know this in order for the program to fulfil its purpose. The goal is to meet the business objective with everyone satisfied. A consultant cannot do this without talking and listening to everyone involved.

Ask all of the above questions and your consultancy assignment will start and finish on firm grounds.

## Interviews With Users

Interviews with users can be less formal than with your client. Using this method, you may get to learn a little more. Many users are wary of being reviewed and checked up upon. Ensure that you spend some time watching what the person does. Ask them to show you how they perform a typical task. Often what they do is entirely different to what the handbook says they should be doing. Humans have a great way in saving time and finding the most comfortable way to do things – they are called "work rounds".

Make sure that you can keep your user comfortable and let them see your notes. Go into the meeting prepared with some structured questions, but be ready to go "off course" if the meeting requires it.

At the end of the meeting you should have a good idea of what your users do, how they do it, how often and why. If you remember What, Why, How and When you will be halfway there.

## Meetings

Meetings are very efficient in obtaining a lot of information very quickly as long as they are well structured and tightly managed. Meetings can have one of the following aims:

- Communication - what is going on?
- Informative - what is happening? Broadcasting news e.g. company changes, product launches
- Presenting a proposal - how we want to do it?
- Progress - what we have done so far? Results of a survey presented.
- Fact finding - obtain information.

For a successful meeting you should invite:

- The person/people who CAN make the decisions that you require to be made.
- People involved in decision making process.
- People who hold KEY information required during the meeting.

- People who may be affected by any decisions being made.
- People who NEED to be involved.

Inviting any more people will quickly mean that the meeting becomes unmanageable and you will not be able to find the information you require and/or obtain the decisions you need.

**Steps to organising and effective meeting**

- **Prepare** yourself.
- **Organise** your meeting.
- **Manage** your meeting.
- **Record** your meeting.
- **Summarise** and collate requirements.

**Prepare** yourself:

- Identify the aim of the meeting.
- Decide what you want to talk about.
- Decide the information you require.
- Review various scenarios.
- Identify your attendees.
- Collect the things together that you will require in the meeting.

**Organise** your meeting:

- Prepare questions, scenarios, options or proposals and send them out if required.
- Plan and prepare agenda.
- Identify appropriate venue.
- Identify chair person (if necessary) and ensure that they are prepared for the meeting.
- Inform attendees.
- Send agenda and meeting objectives.
- Verify attendance.
- Ensure attendees are prepared.
- Ensure items needed in the meeting are available e.g. white board, projector.

**Manage** your meeting:

- Come prepared.
- Open the meeting, stating objectives and timings.
- Ensure Chair person manages meeting.
- Keep to agenda, but be flexible.
- Manage the questions and responses so that no one dominates the meeting or it goes off course.

**Record** your meeting:

- Document all decisions and actions.
- Document all requirements or changes to be made.
- Document all information that you receive.

**Summarise** and collate requirements from:

- The minutes.
- Notes taken from meeting.
- Discussions surrounding the meeting.
- Your own interpretation of events.

## Questionnaires

This are one of the most common methods of collecting information when you have a large number of users that all need to have their ideas included. A questionnaire is typically a list of appropriate questions used within data gathering in the following cases:

- Either as a prompt or as a control on the uniformity of questions asked when you meet people face to face.
- To take a large statistical survey.
- When you have a large number of people to contact and there are too many to meet all of them individually.
- When you require a consensus of opinion.
- When you need a top level overview of the roles within a department.
- When you wish to remove any subtle influences from the questions asked.

Some typical advantages are:

- They save time taken in meeting many people.
- You reach many users at the same time.
- They provide a uniformity of questions.

The disadvantages are:

- Production, distribution, collection, monitoring and collation can be lengthy and complex.
- The return of questionnaires is spasmodic.
- Need non biased, non assisted questions.
- Some "side information" not gathered.
- People may have a fear of putting their opinions in writing.
- No guidance and assistance is available to the user.
- They can be seen as a threat sometimes.
- Questionnaires cannot replace actually watching activities and talking to users.

**Remember:** WHAT, WHERE, WHEN, WHY and HOW, when setting up your questions.

The simpler your questionnaire is the more likely it is to be completed. So use multiple choice, tick boxes and discrete questions wherever possible.

## Walkthroughs

Walkthroughs are when you follow a piece of data, information or document through its entire business process in order to:

- Document its path.
- Identify any changes or duplications.
- Identify any breakdown in the flow.
- Identify any doubling of effort.

Advantages:

- Gives clear indication of entire life of a document or piece of data.
- Identifies any problem areas.
- Identifies possible consolidations of effort.
- Can be used to trail a possible solution.

Disadvantages:

- Can be a lengthy or complex task.
- Can be disruptive to normal working life.

It is best to undertake this activity on known problem areas or when processes or procedures are being changed.

You do this by identifying the starting place for a piece of information. This would be such activities as a phone call, letter or other customer interaction. Looking at technology, it could be a computer output or when some information is required for a specific activity.

Go to the first person that has this piece of data/information or paper and then follow the information through the company listing the following:

- Who had the information, when, why and how.
- What they did with it.
- How it changed.
- What other data, information or paper was involved.
- Who they handed it off to and under what circumstances.

At the end of this activity you should have a perfect data flow diagram and set of information.

## Process Mapping and Data Flow Diagrams

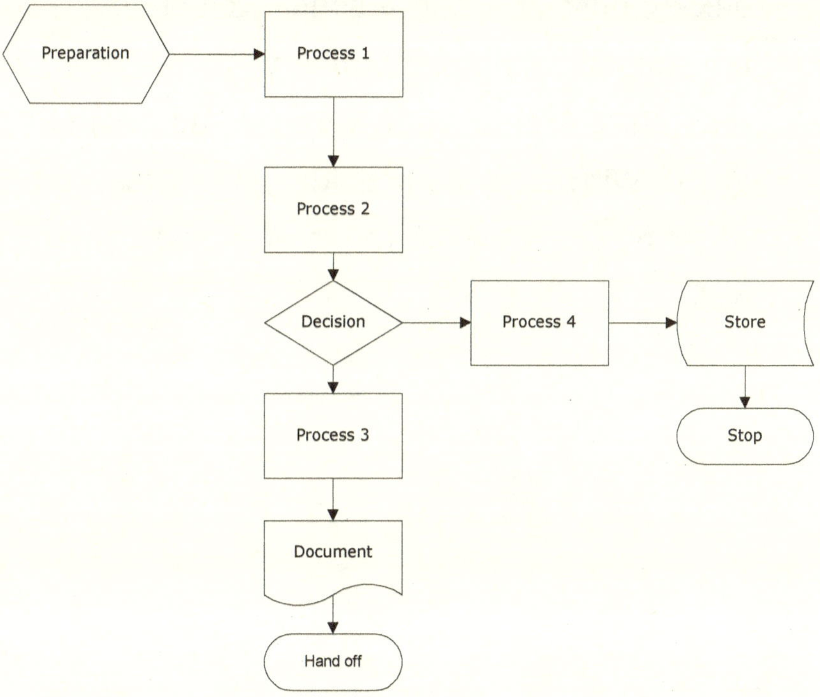


Above is a fairly simple process diagram which identifies the various actions that can happen to a piece of data, information or paper.

This diagram would be accompanied by a bullet point list of what happens at each point of the diagram. Once you have a series of these, you can quickly identify loops, duplication of activity and omissions. The process diagram can be quickly built up using a simple template that can be purchased from stationery shops. You can then place it onto a software package such as Ms Visio. With complex activities, it is usual to build up a macro view of the office environment as well.

## Workshops

Workshops are a subtly controlled but free flowing way of obtaining analytical information from a group of people. The are managed and subtly controlled by the consultant and used to brain storm or think tank. Problems or scenarios are described and comments invited - ideas cascade with the copious use of whiteboards and flip charts. Proceedings are free flowing, all comments are displayed and any ideas are documented.

Advantages:

- Once confidence is gained, they are an excellent way of obtaining ideas and data that may otherwise not be available.
- They are non judgmental if managed correctly.
- Everyone gets a say and can make a difference to the future.
- Fun and productive.

Disadvantages:

- Must be well managed so that all are heard.
- May be difficult getting all the people together.
- There will be lot of data to correlate and document.
- Very tiring for the consultant - allow at least one day organisation and one day collation for every day of the workshop.
- It must be well managed in order to collect the information needed in a friendly and enjoyable manner.

The organisation of a workshop is very similar to that of a meeting, except that instead of an agenda a set of aims are provided. Running the workshop should allow it to be free running but with some control so that it does not go too of course. It may help to introduce some scenarios to explore.

## Prototypes

Prototypes are models of a part or all of a system, presented to the client for their opinions and comments, in advance of full development.

There are two types:

- To be developed or incorporated into the final system - used for Rapid Application Development (RAD) or for incremental development.
- To be discarded after review and only used to demonstrate potential

They are used because they:

- Identify, clarify and verify the user's requirements.
- Assist the evaluation of the system functionality.
- Demonstrate the developer's understanding of the required "look and feel" of the system.
- Lessen the impact of the full system implementation.

- They are a controlled and efficient method of iterative and staged implementation.

Advantages:

- Demonstrate progress.
- Aid communication between users and developers.
- Once confidence is gained, they are an excellent way of obtaining ideas and data that may otherwise not be available
- Encourage and support the formulation of the detailed system requirements.
- Enable users to become familiar with the system on an incremental basis.

Disadvantages:

- They can be costly and time consuming - especially if they do not have the desired effect.
- Diverts resources from main project.

So make them pertinent and effective.

## Report Writing

As the consultant you will be doing a lot of report writing. You will need to know how to write a report so that it gives the information that you want to in the way that you want to. Report writing how you get your observations and proposals into a suitable package and is usually the deliverable at the end of a consultancy term.

### Building the Report - Pegs and Strings

**Tell them what you are telling them**

**Tell them**

**Tell them why you are telling them**

**Tell them again**

A report should consist of the following:

**Executive Summary**

- Introduction
- Main Body
- Conclusion

The executive summary is read by those that make the major decisions and do not have enough time to go into the finer detail. Ensure that you write your summary for this audience. The executive summary should be a stand-alone document.

**Introduction**

- Aim of Report
- Scope and Objectives
- Business Requirements

This is the "tell them what you are telling them" part of your report.

☞Each Business Requirement is now a peg.

**Main Body**

- Options
- Proposals
- Risks
- Costs

This is the "tell them" part.

☞From each peg hangs a string that can be followed through from each peg above.

## Conclusion

This is the "Tell them why you are telling them" part.

## Recommendations

This is the "Tell them again" part.

☞Each string follows through to the Recommendations

☞Thus, a subject within the report can be followed logically through the report

## Packaging the Report

It must have the following:

- Executive summary that stands alone and includes requirements, proposals and recommendations.
- Glossary if there is a complex terminology.
- Graphics to aid understanding of more complex areas.
- Be concise and to the point.
- Should be well presented.

## Reports Presentation

It is often necessary to present your report, particularly if it is a deliverable that will result in you being paid. When presenting your conclusion:

- Send advance copy.
- Make an appointment to present the report.
- If informal then you will just need read it through or summarise.
- Arrange to leave copies as appropriate.

## Formal Presentation:

- Know your aims.
- Know your audience.
- Choose appropriate presentation material.
- Graphics always help.
- Plan, practice and time.
- Obtain feedback.
- Reach conclusions, agreement.

## Sign Off

A sign off is very important - it is what gets you an agreement to your report and eventually gets you paid!

## Business Case

A good business case is usually key to a company obtaining funding for a project. As a consultant you will spend a lot of time defining a business case. The business case:

- Is the justification for undertaking a project?
- Defines the benefits that the system is expected to deliver.
- Shows the savings that will accrue, measured against the cost of implementing and running the system.
- Identifies the risks that will be run and what will be done to mitigate them.

A complete business case should include the following:

- **Achievability** — Do all involved have the ability, experience, expertise, and resources to complete the project? Do you have the appropriate approach to overcome any potential obstacles, e.g. resource needs, timelines, or budgets?

- **Assumptions** — Check with all the stakeholders and major players in the project, that they have similar assumptions and that they are valid.
- **Scope** – Define what is in/out of scope with the existing budget and resources.
- **Benefits** - Define the benefits and opportunities that each option provides. Identify those that align with the company's business objectives and ensure that they can be measured.
- **Critical Success Factors** — Establish with the stakeholders what will be identified as a success and how this will be measured. It is important to understand their expectations and establish the deliverables of the project. This success factors should be specific, identifiable measurable and achievable.
- **Risks** – Capture all anticipated risks – plan contingencies. Prepare a high-level estimate of the costs for each risk. Look at the impact that delaying the project or under-delivering could have.

- **Dependencies** – Identify the internal e.g. staff availability, and external dependencies, e.g. changes in the marketplace, new government legislation. Projects that are dependent upon and who depend on this project should also be identified.
- **Options** - Include details of all available options that could meet the business needs. The usual number is three to five, including the "do nothing" option. Consider the costs, benefits and risks associated with each option, and the degree to which each option meets the project's needs. Make sure that you have included the overall supply chain's needs, i.e. the organization, partners, suppliers, staff and customers.
- **Costs** – Establish the costs for each option and establish who pays what and when. You may want to factor in 10-20% for potential problems. Establish if the costs are appropriate for the amount of returns and risks undertaken.

- **Resources** — Identify those individuals, units, and departments who are involved and/or affected by the project. Scope the anticipated resource and capabilities requirements that you will need, such as staff, IT, workspace, equipment, and funding.
- **Stakeholders** — Identify their role, responsibility, availability and contingencies if they become incapacitated or released from the project.

Once you have checked off these points, your business case should be ready to send to the project stakeholders. You should then look at:

- **Strategic fit** - Confirm that the project is still required and that its objectives are still in line with the company's business goals.
- **Procurement** — Send an Invitation to Tender (ITT) to prospective contractors. Evaluate their bids. Hold presentations with the most impressive bids and then choose the winning bid.

## Feasibility Study

A Feasibility Study is a report investigating the feasibility, risks, rewards and options of undertaking a course of action or project. The report should consist of:

- **Term of reference** - Why, what and how you are doing it?
- **Scope and objectives** - How wide the study is - what is not covered, what you are hoping to achieve?
- **Business requirements** - To address business problems, changes and wishes.
- **Business case** - What will be gained by the business for addressing the business requirements?
- **SWOT analysis** - Strengths, weaknesses, opportunities, threats arising from undertaking/not undertaking project.
- **Options available** - What options are available including the "do nothing" option?

- **Cost benefit analysis** - Costs and benefits for each option.
- **Impact and effects** - What will happen, to what and how if the options are undertaken?
- **Recommendations**- What happens now?

You need to assess the viability of the proposed system with respect to the following:

- Will it meet the Business Requirement?
- Is the risk of undertaking the project acceptable?
- Is the required system and technical architecture appropriate to present technology?
- Are the proposed budget and resources appropriate?
- Are the costs of the system and it is operating costs justified?
- Will the system meet the user's expectations and requirements?
- Will the system save the clients money and make them more profitable?

- Will the system improve productivity and efficiency?
- Will the system provide better management information allowing better decisions to be taken
- Investigating the feasibility, risks, rewards and options of undertaking a course of action or project.

## Feasibility Tasks

### Business Requirement

- Interviews, discussions and consultations with proposed sponsors, senior users and budget providers to ascertain and agree the Business Requirement.
- The formal definition of the problem faced by a business and the justification for requiring the system, an outline of the benefits that will accrue, the savings it will bring.

**Term of Reference**

- The definition of the scope of the work to be undertaken by the consultants and project team, together with the project's time and resource allocations.

**Scope and Objectives**

- The definition of the objectives for a project, background, reasons and constraints on the solution.

**Business Case**

- The justification for undertaking a project, defining the benefits that the system is expected to deliver, the savings it will accrue, measured against the cost of implementing and running the system and the risks that will be run.

**SWOT Analysis**

- Undertake a SWOT (Strengths, Weaknesses, Opportunities, and Threats) analysis on the system, proposals and Business Requirement.

**Risk Analysis**

- Ascertain and measure the risks associated with each option.

**Impact**

- Ascertain any constraints that may be placed upon the project or the system.

**Cost Benefit Analysis**

- Obtain outline costs guesstimates (± 30%)
- Define at least four options, including "no action" to meet the Business Requirement
- Ascertain and measure the benefits associated with each option. Ensure that tangible and intangible benefits are documented
- Ascertain and measure the costs associated with each option. Ensure that tangible and intangible costs are documented.
- Prepare a cost benefit analysis (CBA) from the above actions.

**Project Organization and Structure**

- Outline of the project organization and structure will be.

**Initial Planning**

- Outline macro analysis of the site, existing system, problems and solutions presently being considered.
- Outline macro level discussions with senior users.
- Macro walkthrough and outline document flow diagram of existing system

**Authorisation**

- Prepare, present and obtain formal sign off of documentation.
- Obtain sign off to proceed to next stage.

> **Note: at this stage you are investigating the feasibility of the proposed system and not producing an outline system design.**

## The User Requirement Specification

The User Requirement Specification (USR) will often be a major deliverable of your consultancy consignment. It is a report, that, as the name suggests, contains all the user requirement in great detail. For ease of understanding Business Requirements are at a macro level whereas User Requirements are at a micro level.

Ask yourself: What does the user need to change/acquire if we are to go ahead with meeting the business requirement.

WHAT WHY WHEN HOW WHERE

Examples:

- What happens when?
- Why do you want this?
- When wills this happen?
- How do you do this?
- Where is the best place for this action?

When searching for requirements look at changes arising from the:

- Organisation – is the organisation making major changes? Organisation structural changes, mergers, changes in sales, expansion and consolidation.
- Business – are the products or the markets changing? Is there a change in strategy or is technology forcing new changes?
- Buyers- are they moving into new markets or are the users becoming more sophisticated?
- Users – is there new training, new processes and procedures?
- System- is the system outdated, software being upgraded not meeting new business changes? Is greater security needed or has new technology forced upgrades?
- Jobs are they being eliminated, created, transferred or are there going to be changed responsibilities?

Changes from the organisation, business, user and system are all interdependent.

Requirements are gathered and then more deeply defined and refined as the project moves on as the user's perspective of the new system requirements becomes much clearer.

**The User Requirement Specification**

This is the formal documentation of all the agreed user requirements and must be signed off by the sponsor as acceptable. It should consist of:

- Introduction
- User requirements
- Acceptance criteria
- Sign off by sponsor as acceptable

The introduction should encompass:

- A brief overview of the deliverable or project.
- Who has been consulted.
- The reason for the report.

User requirements should be

- Easily identifiable.
- Aligned to the business objectives.
- Reflect a consensus of opinion.

- Be technically feasible.
- Meet and fit in with the company culture.

Acceptance criteria must be:

- Available for each requirement.
- Be measurable either quantifiably or a measurement of quality.
- Be readily understood.
- Be well enough defined for testing and acceptance purposes.

The sign off by sponsor as acceptable is the most important part of the report

As the name suggests, it establishes the baseline of the Project Requirements - all other changes are made through Change Control

It is the fully documented and agreed User Requirements which defines the following:

- The Business Requirement.
- The proposed budget and resources.
- The proposed costs of the system and it's operating costs.

- The required system and technical architecture appropriate to present technology.

It defines the system and processes to:

- Meet the User's expectations and requirements.
- Save the clients money and make them more profitable.
- Improve productivity and efficiency.
- Provide better management information allowing for better decisions to be taken.

Unlike the Project Plan, it is ***not*** a living document and remains unchanged throughout the life of the project.

**Report Contents**

- Executive Summary.
- Computer Strategy.
- Business Constraints and Dependencies.
- System Objectives.

- Existing Workflow. This section should document the existing workflow and operating procedures related to the project. Where applicable this text may be supported by use of suitable diagrams.
- Proposed Workflow. This section documents the proposed workflow and operating procedures, highlighting the processes that will require further development. Where applicable this text may be supported by use of suitable diagrams (DFD, ERD etc.)

**So, What Are User Requirements?**

They are the documentation of any changes required of the organisation, business, user and system and are interdependent.

Organisation structural changes:

- Mergers, sales etc.
- Expansion and consolidation.
- Jobs eliminated, created, transferred.
- Changed responsibilities.

Business changes:

- Market changes.
- Internal changes.
- Strategy changes.
- Technological changes.

User based changes:

- Procedures and processes.
- Training.
- Technology transfer.

System technical changes

- Hardware.
- Software: functionality, interfaces, dependencies.
- Network.
- Maintenance and support.
- Housekeeping and audit.
- Security.

## Work Flow Analysis

Workflow analysis is the top-level activity undertaken to review how a packet of work moves through the business from start to inception. A packet of work is something like "taking customer contact information over the phone". Sometimes it is easier to follow data. Start with where the phone is answered - go to how the information is gathered and noted and then finish at where the information is finally stored for future use. (This point is called the hand-off).

## Processes and Procedures

Processes are WHAT are being done and procedures are HOW it is being done.

An example of a process would be: open a new customer account.

An example of a procedure would be: ascertain name; ascertain contact details; etc.

How do we document them?

- Use a workflow template available from many stationary stores - difficult to update.
- Use a software programme such as Visio.
- Use a graphics programme such as PowerPoint - difficult to use.

**How Do We Do It?**

- Identify each activity.
- Identify what happens.
- Identify who does it.
- Identify how one activity connects to the next one.
- Document them all.
- You should end up with a line of activities connected to each other.
- You SHOULD have a start and an end - if you do not go back and sort it out!.

The correct use of this procedure will highlight:

- Double handling - data handled more than once for the same task, or data going to more than one entity.
- Loops in the system - a route taken more than once.
- Holes in the system - items or actions not covered or undertaken.
- Gaps in the system - lack of continuation of information flow.
- Inefficient handling - consolidation of one or more actions or data elements will speed the system.
- Lack of audit trail - no traceable path of actions taken.
- Poor security - lack of appropriate precautions.
- Poor housekeeping - inefficient housekeeping or storage routines .
- Inappropriate actions - illegal or unofficial actions, or those inappropriate to the task.
- Inappropriate actioner - task person has inappropriate skills or grade.

Taking each process you can build up a view of what is happening within the business and where any problems may be.

A few points to remember:

- Your reports should be pertinent, readable and aimed at your audience.
- Forget jargon - your role, as a business analyst is to write for the business in their language.
- The sign off by sponsor as acceptable is the most important part of the report.

## Organisational Analysis

Organisational Analysis, the most well known analysis structure used was first designed and developed by McKinsey and Co. It is known as the "Seven S's".

- **Structure:** - how is the business currently organised?
- **Strategy:** - how has the company decided to achieve it's goals?
- **Systems:** - what business procedures, processes and IT platforms influence and constrain the organisation?
- **Skills**: What is the competence of the organisation?
- **Style**: In what manner does the management present itself to its staff and how does the company present itself to the world?
- **Super-ordinate goals**: What philosophy and values does the company uphold and work towards?

- **Staff:** the quality of the people within the company – directors, management and employees?

By documenting and reviewing the structure of the company or affected business areas and applying the "Seven S's" an understanding of:

- What changes should be recommended.
- What changes will/can be made under the new regime.
- Where any weaknesses are.

Other documents and analysis tools you will come across

- **Functional Specification** - A technical specification and description of the proposed system.
- **Document Flow Diagrams** - A diagrammatic description of each document and how it moves (flows) through the existing and proposed system. Details of changes enacted upon each document.

- **Data Flow Diagrams (DFD):** Similar to the Document Flow Diagram except that the flow of each piece of data appertaining to the documents and the system is described.
- **Entity Relationship Diagrams (ERD):** A diagrammatic description of each small part (entity) of the system interacts with other parts of the system.
- **Entity Life History (ELH):** A diagrammatic description of each small part (entity) of the system interacts and changes over the life span of the system.

## Cost Benefit Analysis

Cost Benefit Analysis is to measure and weigh the benefits against the risks and costs of proceeding with the proposed activity, project or consultancy assignment. The activities involved should be:

- Interviews, discussions and consultations with proposed sponsors, senior users and budget providers.
- Outline macro analysis of the site, existing system, problems and solutions presently being considered.
- Outline macro level discussions with senior users.
- Macro walk through and outline document flow diagram of existing system.
- Obtain outline costs guesstimates (± 30%).
- Define at least four options, including "no action" to meet the Business Requirement.
- Ascertain and measure the risks associated with each option.

- Ascertain and measure the benefits associated with each option. Ensure that tangible and intangible benefits are documented.
- Ascertain and measure the costs associated with each option. Ensure that tangible and intangible costs are documented.
- Prepare a cost benefit analysis (CBA) from the above three actions.
- Prepare, present and obtain formal sign off of documentation.

## SWOT

A SWOT analysis is an excellent way of looking at a business from a macro view point. The SWOT analysis stands for:

- Strengths
- Weaknesses
- Opportunities
- Threats

Strengths and weaknesses are the internal factors of your business. Opportunities and threats are external factors that affect your business. Investigate the various SWOT's and grade them. There are two ways to do this – pictorial and numerical.

**Pictorial:** First of all get a large writing pad and put a large + in the centre of the page. Then put the titles Strengths, Weakness, Opportunities and Threats around the cross – one in each sector. Place each of the SWOT's so that the more troublesome the problem is, the farther away from the + you place it.

The better the factor then the closer to the + you place it. View the grid and look at solving the outlaying problems first. The tighter the display is to the centre of the + - the better shape your business is in.

| **Strengths** | **Weaknesses** |
|---|---|
| X Good price point<br>X Skilled staff | X Low market share |
| **Opportunities** | **Threats** |
| Fashion X<br>X New products | X Technology changes<br>X Manufacturing costs |

Thus, this option has a fair strength, very few weaknesses, some opportunities and some threats. As you build up the table – your options should become clearer. The more the options are to the center – the better.

**Numerical:** Give each item a rating from 1 to 5 as to its importance to your business with 5 being the most important. Also give each factor a rating from A to E as to its impact on your business, with E being the highest impact. Now investigate all the E's and 5's if they are bad factors then change or mitigate them. If they are strengths and opportunities then build upon them. Obviously the more high strengths and opportunities combined with low weaknesses and threats the better your business is.

| Item | Importance | Impact |
|---|---|---|
| Good price point | 3 | B |
| Skilled staff | 4 | A |
| Low market share | 5 | A |
| Fashion | 2 | C |
| New products | 3 | C |
| Technology changes | 4 | B |
| Manufacturing costs | 5 | C |

As mentioned above, strengths and weaknesses are internal factors and they can be found in the following:

1. **Management structure:** such factors as relying too much on the owner. Needing more managers etc.
2. **Your workforce:** including employee turnover and difficulty of finding skilled staff.
3. **Sales:** strength of sales, how reliant your sales are on external factors (think ice cream seller), cyclical sales.
4. **Operations:** your internal efficiency, speed of manufacture or delivery.
5. **Financial:** cash flow, time to collect on invoices, ease of obtaining loans.

Your opportunities and threats can be found in the following categories:

1. **Threats of new entrants to your market:** Could a big box retailer open up near your business. Do you hold a patent that puts a brake on competitors?

2. **Supplier's bargaining power:** Can you suppliers force you to take large deliveries. Are suppliers difficult to find? Is supply readily available?
3. **Customer's influence:** Do you rely on just a few customers? Can some of your customers insist on lower prices? Do you have a lot of late payers?
4. **Competitors:** Is competition very strong? Do you have a near monopoly?
5. **Substitution:** Are there numerous other products that could be purchased rather than your? How unique or superior are your offerings?

So why do this? Well going through this exercise forces you to look deeply into the current and potential business. It also provides a model of how strong the business is and areas that you should be concentrating on. Well thousands of business consultants can't be wrong!

## Other Business Analysis Techniques

There are other techniques that can be used in the analysis of processes, data and situations. Some of them are detailed below.

### PESTLE

This method is for the analysis of external factors that may affect an organisation. The work PESTLE is taken from the six areas that are investigated.

- **P**olitical - current and potential influences from political pressures.
- **E**conomic – the impact of the local, national and world economy.
- **S**ociological -how a society can affect an organisation, the measure of sociological pressures. Particularly used in medical and science environments.
- **T**echnological -the effect of new and emerging technology on the business.

- **L**egal - the effect of national and world legislation on the business.
- **E**nvironmental -the impact of local, national and world environmental issues on the business.

**MOST**

This is a check on a current project to see that it is still aligned to four attributes – typically called MOST after their initials.

- **M**ission - where the business intends to move to.
- **O**bjectives - the key goals which will help achieve the mission.
- **S**trategies – the options chosen to move the business forward.
- **T**actics – how the strategies will be put into action.

## CATWOE

This process is used to review what the business is trying to achieve and how it affects the people involved. It can also be used to consider the impact of any proposed solution on these same people. CATWOE refers to the six types of people and processes involved in most businesses.

- **C**ustomers - who are the beneficiaries of the highest level business process and how does the issue affect them?
- **A**ctors – who are involved in the situation? Who will be involved in implementing solutions and what will the impact be on their success?
- **T**ransformation Process - what processes or systems are affected by the issue?
- **W**orld View - What is the bigger picture and the wider impacts of the issue?
- **O**wner - Who owns the process or situation being investigated and what role will they play in the solution?

- **E**nvironmental Constraints - What are the constraints and limitations that will impact upon the solution and its success?

As can be seen by reviewing the processes, they are good aid memoirs for questions that you need to ask during most business analysis sessions.

## Business Process Improvement

Business Process Improvement (BPI) is a systematic approach to improving the efficiency of a company by improving the way that it works.

Michael Hammer defines business process reengineering (BPR), in his book *Reengineering the Corporation* as:
*"Fundamental rethinking and radical redesign of business processes to bring about dramatic improvements in performance."*

BPR is the much more radical change of the entire business, whilst BPI is the change of the processes within the business. Both BPI and BPR look at the five basic components of a business:

- Strategy
- Processes
- Technology
- Organization
- Culture

BPI typically involves six steps:

1. **Selection of the process team.** These teams are small of usually no more than 4 people, including a leader.
2. **Training the team.** This involves techniques and documentation - both of which are very important. This is to ensure that the analysis is uniform and efficient.
3. **Interviews with the uses.** Working methodically and chasing the process through the company, the users are interviewed. During these interviews it is important that each process as well as what prompts the process to be started as well as the "handoff" to other processes are captured. It is important to capture the process as it is performed as opposed to how it is supposed to be performed.
4. **Collation of the documentation.** The processes should now be reviewed and integrated so that a process map is built. This is a macro view of all the processes and how they all interact.

At this point process improvements can start to be identified. If possible an improved process map should also be started.

5. **Reviews and rewrites.** The draft process map and process documentation should be reviewed, people re-interviewed if necessary and the process map improved. This could happen several times and should be treated as an iterative process.
6. **Problem analysis.** During 4 and 5 problems will be identified, gaps and overlaps identified and better methods to do things.

Now you have two process maps –one containing the existing processes, the second the streamlined, more efficient processes. Now it becomes a project to move the business from one map to the next – that is the difficult part.

## Managing Change

Change is often a difficult processes for many people and as a consultant you will often be called upon to manage change. The higher up the management ladder you work at, the harder change management is and often your experience of managing change is what is being paid for. Here is an outline of the different kinds of changes you will find.

**Major changes** are those that will make a significant impact upon resources, budget, time scales, project plan or existing development or hardware configuration. Major changes will usually impact upon time scales, costs and sometimes contracts- for example a major database structure change.

**Minor changes** are those that have an insignificant impact upon the proposed system or project plan and will take minimal implementation - for example a help-screen change.

**Planned changes** are those that are anticipated within the project plan - for example a new version or release of software.

**Unplanned changes** are not within the existing project plan and usually originate from the user or from discovered error- for example a request for more system functionality or a correction of an error found in testing.

**Anticipated changes** may not necessarily be within the existing project plan, but they usually originate from consultancy and analysis discussions or from a proposal made by the Consultant - fore example hardware, configuration change to take advantage of newly emerged technology.

**Unanticipated changes** are by far the worst kind, and usually signal poor project management or client relationship, both of which should highlight any possible requests or future requirements.

Should an unanticipated change be requested, remedial action should be immediately taken to regain awareness of user's needs and control of the project. They can originate from user, project team, quality reviews or testing.

## Seminars

Seminars are a great way of earning money and a great skill to learn. You can either hold seminars to promote your own business or as part of your consultancy offering.

## Setting Up Your Seminar

In any seminar, there are basic pieces of information that an audience should receive from their presenter. You are the problem solver presenting a solution that will benefit your audience. The presentation should answer who, what, when, where, why and how regarding your topic. In giving that information, your presentation will have clarity and will be on track to give the detail necessary to your audience.

**Who - Who is your target audience?** What would they like to know about regarding your presentation? Do they have any preconceived notions about your material? What are their concerns?

Are you addressing the "who" you targeted in your research? When you address the "who" of your message, you are better able to relate with your audience. They will feel like you are speaking directly to them. They will give you their attention because they feel like their needs are being addressed.

**What - What is the message you want to communicate?** What are the issues? What are the solutions? The "what" in your message is the backbone of your presentation. It is your purpose of your message and the reason you are speaking. It is also the reason why people come to hear you.

**When - When is the recommended time to take action?** Is there a sense of urgency in your presentation? Stressing the "when" aspect of your message is especially important when you want your audience to take action immediately following the presentation - i.e. - sign up for a class, sell promotional materials, implement what was learned)

**Where - Where is the problem located?** Where can your audience find the help they need? "Where" signifies direction. This leads your audience somewhere in your presentation. Where would you like to take them? Common "where" statements include "across America today", "in college campuses nationwide", "in the construction industry", and "in families in California".

**Why - Why should they take action?** What are the motivating factors in prompting your audience to take action? The main focus here is inspiration and motivation to take action. Not only do you want them to listen to you, but you want your audience to take action on what you've said. You want to somehow improve their lives and honing your message on the "why" is a critical necessity.

**How - How can they respond to your message?** How can they take action based on what they've heard? This is the learning and teaching portion of your message.

This can be the "how-to" section telling them how they can easily improve their lives. This section often incorporates steps to follow.

As you piece all of these bits of information together, you'll be giving your audience the detailed answers they are looking for. You also present yourself as the credible source of information you want to present yourself to be!

## Organising Your Seminar

One of the most difficult aspects of making your presentation is getting started. You may be feeling overwhelmed even if you have been working with your materials for years but the first step is to jump in there and get started.

**Research your material.** Collect and read as much information as possible. Make some notes and also look at the validity of the information you are collecting. Is the information outdated? Is it relevant to the actual subject you are going to talk about? Start taking notes and highlighting potentially key points of your presentation.

**Review.** Once you feel you've gathered enough information to present, review your notes and select the information you are going to present. Look for key ideas that support the purpose of your talk. Decide how deep you will go when presenting your information? Consider your audience. What do they need to know to take action on your subject? How much detail do they actually need? Consider also, the length of the time you'll have for your presentation.

**Organize your key ideas into an outline form.** Start with the key points you will make and add two to three supporting elements to it. When you speak, you will be leading your audience from point A to point B. You are taking them somewhere even if it's only in their minds. Does your outline show a path to take? Is it relevant? Adjust your key points until you do lead your audience to where you want them to go.

**Decide how you will present your organised information in your presentation.** What visual aids can you use to strengthen your points? Is there data or research that you can bring into your presentation? How can you vary the delivery of your message? Your presentation will be more interesting if you do more than just talk. People can easily tune out of your message especially if it is during a meal or immediately following one.

**Organize your presentation outline** to incorporate your visuals and method of delivery in your presentation. Review what it looks like on paper. Your outline is like your map for success. Is your map clearly defining the information you want to say? Are there any weak points were the information is not as strong as you'd like it to be? If it's not, revise and review and keep doing this until you get your map the way you want it to be.

Organising the material for your presentation is a process. As you take your audience from lack of knowledge to having knowledge, create an seminar outline map of the journey. This map is the key to your success and the only way to be successful is to have a plan of action.

## Charisma Matters!

If you want to take your consulting expertise on the road, then offering seminars may be just the ticket. Of course, you will need to do more than just present a dry recitation of facts and figures. Like any type of public figure who takes center stage for an event, you have to be able to hold the attention of your audience. In short, you need to have a good dose of charisma.

Charisma means different things to different people. But at the end of the day, it is the result of your charisma that you want to focus on.

You want people to listen to you. You want people to trust you. You want people to respect you enough to put your suggestions into action. Basically, you want people to like you.

Cultivating your coaching persona can mean taking on several attributes. It is a good idea to make sure those attributes come naturally to you. Otherwise you come off as artificial and stilted at best, or just plain phony at worst. Here are some attributes that are likely to help you hold the attention of the audience:

- **Humor**. No, you don't have to dress like a clown or constantly tell jokes in order to be humorous - unless that is relevant to the seminar! But humor has a way of helping people to relax and enjoy what is going on around them. A little humor scattered through your presentation will help people to settle in and be comfortable enough to absorb all that wonderful education you are providing.

- **Verbiage**. While technical terms may be necessary up to a point, you also want to keep your presentation accessible to a wide audience. To some extent, you want the presentation to be more like a conversation between friends, and less like a lecture in a college classroom. Using this approach helps people settle down and digest what you are saying in easy bites that go down very easy.
- **Accessibility.** If at all possible, make sure there are ways for people to ask questions or make comments. Vary this a little by providing both time for people to verbally pose a question or offer a comment, and also some means of doing so in a private manner. For example, you can provide pads and pencils that people can write down questions. Instruct them to fold the paper in half and drop them into a receptable when leaving the conference room for a break. Nobody has to know who asked the question in this manner.

All these qualities will translate well into conducting seminars via a web conference. Thus, you really do not have to change your basic style when moving from one medium to another. This helps you be the same person all the time, which is less of a strain on maintaining your persona, and also helps people to see you as being real no matter what the setting happens to be.

## Tips to Overcoming Stage Fright

The first thing you need to understand about stage fright is that it is not uncommon at all. Some of the greatest actors, politicians and other public figures known to society experience the phenomenon every time they get in front of an audience. In short, stage fright is a perfectly rational and human response to a social situation.

For most people, that initial level of anxiety quickly subsides once on stage and into the business at hand.

However, if you find that your stage fright tends to linger, there are a few different tricks you can employ in order to help things along and focus on the business at hand.

First, remind yourself people do not die of stage fright. When is the last time you personally knew someone fainting from stage fright? Chances are you don't, in spite of what you see in the movies or have heard about from vague sources.

The truth is that the anxiety of stage fright is simply a little extra adrenalin coursing through your system. Your body is a wonderful device that knows how to shut down the adrenalin flow before there is too much. So realize that if you don't feed the anxiety by thinking it will never end, your initial bout will be over in just a few minutes.

Second, forget about making a fool of yourself in front of other people. This is the foundation for most cases of stage fright. Remind yourself that you are prepared and you are a professional.

You know how to do this right. Because you are in control, you will not embarrass yourself. Instead, people are expecting to learn something and will inn fact be very happy to be in your presence for the course of your time on stage.

Last, pick out a few people around the audience to address. While your remarks are intended for everyone present, identifying a few faces that seem to be especially welcoming will help to trick your brain into thinking in terms of having a conversation with just a handful of people – a much less anxious situation for most people.

As you calm down and get into the swing of your presentation, you will quickly find you are having that private conversation with more and more people.

One final word of advice – don't dread stage fright. It is a useful tool that will help you to stay mentally alert and on top of things.

That is why many stage actors get really nervous if they don't experience stage fright before stepping onto the stage for the first time that night - they just know their relaxed attitude is going to lead to dropping a line or missing a cue.

So see your initial stage fright as your mind's way of getting you ready to give the best presentation ever!

**Back of the Room Sales?**

Back of the Room Sales are material that are sold in the back of the room, before during or after your seminar. Many audiences like to take information home with them, and Back of the Room products give them this opportunity. What kinds of items make good Back of the Room Sales? Here is a starter list:

- Books.
- CD/DVD sets.
- Study courses.
- Promotional items.
- Other services, such as coaching.

**Books**. This is the most obvious. There is no quicker way to enhance your credibility that to write and publish a book. In some big-city markets, such as Los Angeles, it is difficult if not impossible to secure a speaking engagement without having published a book. But don't let the word publish scare you. Yes, it is lovely if you can get an established New York publisher to bring out your book. However, it is not the only path. It is legitimate to write and publish your own book, and it doesn't even have to be that long. Look into Print on Demand companies. These firms publish books as people order them, one at a time. This is ideal for your website, but can also work for Back of the Room Sales. Simply order several yourself and have them available to look at and if you run out, hand out cards with easy ordering information. Many experts recommend getting a book out as soon as possible, so start writing now!

**CD/DVD sets**. This can be a videotape of your speech, or a longer DVD of your workshops. If you are presenting a keynote seminar, for instance, many people may be interested in your longer presentations and thus buy a DVD of your workshop to take home and watch at their leisure. You can also put some of your training courses onto CD or if you are really organised onto a DVD.

**Study Courses**. As the name implies, a study course is a longer and multi-part publication. It can be on CDs or published style. Often the best study courses are a combination—CD of the material accompanied by a workbook.

**Promotional Items**. Many speakers like to sell or give away pens or pencils or notebooks emblazoned with a catch-phrase or funny quip. Look for items that tie into your presentation. Some speakers develop a collection of small toys or accessories that they sell. Computer consultants may sell mouse pads or other accessories.

**Other services**. One of the most lucrative Back of the Room products can be selling services such as coaching or mentoring sessions. Once audiences have been won over by your wonderful presentations, they are often hungry for more. Many of them would like to work with you and so it will be to your benefit to develop extra services that you can offer.

All of these Back of the Room products are excellent additions to your seminar income. They may not bring in a lot of money, but they are good ways to keep your name in front of people and add credibility. Over time, Back of the Room products can provide you with a nice additional income stream.

## Problems During Consulting

Your clients and users will find project implementation stressful and difficult. The following are the usual reactions to implementation:

- **Impatience** - you have to resist all the pressures of "going live" until the system and the preparations are totally ready.
- **Apprehension** - fear of the unknown or fear of the perceived known. These people must be motivated, reassured and pointed in the right direction.
- **Perfectionism** - you have to decide if the continual testing, checking and communication from your users is a trait of perfectionism, a message that there are problems with you testing and QA controls or a sign that they are unwilling to go live.
- **Being unprepared** - is it poor project management, inadequate training, lack of interest or avoidance of the issues? Again, careful listening and analysis is needed.

- **Lack of support.** Maybe it is not the system the users wanted - they are not ready or are more interested in their current work. Maybe their existing workload is too high. Communication and reassurance, coupled with working to rectify the problems are the weapons here.
- **Unwillingness to Commit** - There is a group of people that are totally unable to make a commitment to any change or decision. Hopefully, by this stage of the project these traits have been identified in your users. Motivation, assurance, training and technology transfer is the answer.
- **Unwillingness to accept responsibility** - again an unfortunate personal trait. Alternatively, is it that the system does not meet the user's requirements? Careful listening and analysis to the reasons and rationale given must be undertaken.

- **Suspicion** of what the implementation will involve. Either it's too good to be true or conversely they are worried that there is a secret agenda - maybe their job or responsibilities will adversely change. Communication and reassurance are the weapons here.
- **Conflict** can arise from fear of the unknown or change. It could also be a signal that the user is not getting what he wanted or expected. In any project implementation, there are always organisational and structural changes within the user business environment. The Consultant must ensure that he overcomes these problems, whilst remaining independent and free from office "politics." A good Consultant must use all their skills and personality to overcome these problems.

- **Lack of interest.** People often find a way of overcoming the failings of a badly designed system, especially when it fails to adapt to required changes. It thus loses user support and approval, which then devise alternative and unofficial systems to cope with the new requirements. The installed system then becomes bypassed, despised and falls into disuse.
- "**We've always done it this way.**" No Consultant has can class himself as experienced until he has heard this phrase at least one hundred times - which is approximately five project implementations.

## Dealing With Difficult Team Members

From time to time, you will get difficult and obstructive people assigned to the team that you are leading. So how do you deal with them? Robert Bramson, author of *Coping with Difficult People*, suggests that you maintain a positive attitude and be direct, descriptive, and non-judgmental. The exception being, of course, when it is a harassment related issue, which needs to be reported to your sponsor immediately.

When dealing with the difficult individual you must remember to do the following:

- Maintain eye contact.
- Monitor the tone of your voice.
- Remain positive and in control of your senses.
- Be direct, descriptive, and non-judgmental.
- Be prepared with the facts.
- Focus on the behaviour and/or issue and do not attack the individual on a personal level.

- Know when to withdraw and report the matter to your consultancy sponsor.
- Look for the root causes of the problem and move beyond the symptoms.
- Do not provoke them into quitting or being fired.
- Do not avoid the situation. It will not go away.

In addition, remember the importance of your reactions, your attitudes, and your response.
Do not expect instant results when dealing with difficult behaviour. Changing behaviour is a long-term process. No technique is going to work overnight. Below are some details about different types of behaviour. You can use this information as a tool to help you effectively deal with the various types of challenging associates

### The Complainer

This individual has a lot of complaints, but few solutions. They use their imagination to create problems. They also appear blameless and innocent.

They also feel like they have to get their personal opinion across and that their personal opinion is fact.

- Find the real problem or the real cause of the problem.
- Avoid accusations.
- Ask specific questions.
- Stick to the facts.
- If their complaints are job-related, determine whether they are unable or unwilling to perform the required tasks.
- Take appropriate action. If you ignore this person, their behaviour will continue to get worse.

**The Back Stabber.**

This person tries to look good by making other people look bad. They try to undermine their leaders and associates in an attempt to make other people look foolish and incompetent. These individuals are passive aggressive, and they will put on a "friendly face" when you are around, but when you are out of sight they will stab you in the back.

- Make it clear that you are aware of their ways.
- Give specific, job related orders.
- Set clear limits regarding behaviour that will not be tolerated.

**The Busybody**

The individual is a professional meddler. They believe that they know everything, but in reality they are typically wrong. They will drop by anytime to gossip and to share their latest bit of gossip.

- Visit with this person privately.
- Show this person how spreading rumours has a negative impact on the team.
- Do not act like as a prosecutor with a hostile witness.
- Keep this individual busy so they have very little time to gossip.
- Focus on the problem, issue, or challenge.

## The "Maybe" Person

This person talks a good game. They have the latest corporate catch phrases down and they know when to use them. However, they typically do not walk their talk. This means that they usually do not produce results. They will tend to procrastinate hoping that a better choice or solution will magically present itself.

- Develop clear and specific objectives.
- Have them commit in advance to the deadlines in the future.
- Make expectations clear.
- Seek the other causes.
- Determine what is applicable and take appropriate action.

### The "No" Person

The person can be a perfectionist. They will avoid mistakes at all costs. They will lose hope and share these feelings with everyone when things go wrong. They could also be called dream stealers because they will extinguish hope in their team members, and they will smother all creative sparks.

- Use compassion and patience with this person.
- Utilise this person as a resource for other individuals.
- Set this person up as your personal character builder.
- Let this person hear new ideas.

### The Predator

This person will personally attack team mates. They will avoid the real issues, and they will set others up as "opponents" to impress you (their leader). These individuals have a hard time being objective.

- Establish and maintain a meeting plan to discuss the real issues.
- Do NOT allow the discussion to drift.
- Keep discussions to the point.
- Refocus the conversations as necessary.

### The "Explosive" Associate

This person will "explode" when they feel threatened. They feel as if they must constantly prove they are capable. These people tend to be concrete in their answers and solutions. They will also resist change by opposing any variation in the process. They will also be irritated and impatient if their plans are resisted or questioned.

- Do not expect these associates to be open or willing to change.
- Allow these associates time to cool down after they lose control.
- Show them that you take their opinion and others' seriously, and that there is a need to respect all opinions equally.

## The Bully

This person will bully their way to get what they want. They believe that by embarrassing their team mates they will gain the support of other team members. They will also throw temper tantrums and they will make your leadership qualities.

- Use self-control and be consistent with this person.
- Do NOT let them pressure you into doing what you do not want to do.
- Confront but do NOT oppose their accusations of you.
- Anticipate challenges from this person.
- Practice what to say to this person.
- When responding to this person use caution.
- Set a time to deal with the situation.

## Putting Your Business On The Internet

Just about anyone can put a web site up on the internet and now days it is quite easy. You have two choices as how to set up your website:

-As a shop window for your company, with contact details etc.

-As a fully working site with ecommerce facilities.

Which ever option you choose, you first need a god domain name. Go to a good domain provider like enom, godaddy, namecheap and spend under £10 on a domain. Choose a domain name that has the word T shirt and or printing in it. This will help with your search engine positioning as well as act as a memory jog to your potential customers.

### As A Shop Window

Hop over to hostgator or similar and then buy a monthly hosting account. With that will come a site maker - where you can easily set up a web site using one of thousands of templates. You can add payment processor linkages, forums etc.

The only problem you will have is you want to sell promote or talk about illegal activities, terrorist activities or sex! Also if you want a high usage activity such as MySpace etc.

### As A Full Site

You will probably need to get this especially written and designed for you. Put your project on sites like guru/elance/scriptlance etc and find a competitive quote.

Get yourself a PayPal account or similar so that you can take payment on your web site. This is much more secure and quicker than taking checks.

## Factors To Remember

Always consider your target market when designing your web site. Include some helpful information about your subject matter but nothing that will give away what you are trying to sell! Ensure that your contact details can be freely found and that details of your company and services are clearly set out.

As you will be asking for money before you deliver something – make your potential customer feel comfortable making payment and tell them what will happen next.

Respond to all enquiries and purchases very quickly. If this is difficult then set up an autoresponder to confirm you have received their enquiry/payment and will get back to them within a few hours. Place references that you have received from past

## An Internet Marketing Strategy

Ok, you've got your web site set up, you are sure that it is search engine friendly and you are pretty certain what your customers want. You've identified at least 3 products that you want to promote and you think that they meet your potential customer's needs. So now what?

Well unfortunately the days, that I can remember, of "build it and they will come" have long gone. Unless you promote your web site – no one will know that you are there and no visitors means no sales. So where so you go from here? Well take a deep breath, a pen and paper and let's start on your Marketing Strategy. Briefly for a new business, with a relatively inexperienced marketer, your strategy will probably include the following options:

–Pay Per Click Advertising

–Article Marketing

–Email Marketing

–Community Marketing

–Classified Advertising

So let's get started - and before you start panicking, you are just writing your Marketing Strategy. This chapter will explain how to do all of the following.

**Your Advertising Kit**

For each of your programs/products

1. Write a short advert – say 50 words.
2. Write a very short advert – say 15 words
3. Write a short article – say about 400 – 600 words.
4. Decide on your keywords – say about 30 – 50 words.

**Your Marketing Kit**

For your web site theme

1. Write at least 6 short auto responder messages.
2. Find or write at least 2 giveaway products.

**Your Marketing Tools**

1. Your web site
2. An autoresponder
3. A good email account

Now let's put all of these together into your first Marketing Strategy.

1. **Submit your web site to all the major search engines.** This will start to get your web site noticed. As this takes a long time, it needs to be the first thing that you do. You can do this yourself or pay someone else to do this for you. We provide this service for our customers for £20 a month, which includes submission to Google, Yahoo and MSN.
2. **Set up your autoresponder form** on your web site and load your messages into the autoresponder. Ensure that you offer one of the giveaway products as a bonus for signing onto your ezine. The second giveaway can be set up for message 3 or 4. Your messages should be sent in the following intervals. Day 1,3,7,7,7,7
3. **Set up your download pages**, for your bonus products as well as the products you are selling. Ensure that you provide an extra offer on each download page.

4. **Submit your article** – including your resource box, to about 6 major ezine article sites. Limit yourself to 6 at the moment. Each of these submissions, if accepted will give you a link to your web site. If too many links to your new web site appear very quickly, search engines assume that you have been using "black hat" SEO tactics (a total no no) and will not list your site.
5. **Identify 4 forums** that discuss the topics of your web site. Set yourself up an account name that describes you well. We use the name "Biz Guru" which is our trade mark and name. Set up your signature to include your web site address. You now have 4 good links to your web site.
6. **Answer Questions:** Start answering questions asked within the forums. Do NOT post adverts for your web site or products. Use this time to establish your credentials. If you answer questions well and contribute to the forums, your web site tag will be noticed.

7. **Set up a PPC campaign** – you can start with the smaller search engines first. Take your very small advert and your keywords and use them in your campaign. Most search engines will help you with your choice of keywords. Remember to set a budget and test, test and test again until you get quality and converting traffic.
8. **Set up some classified ads**. You can do this one of two ways: i) choose one or two major sites/email lists and advertise with them. ii) use an ezine ad blaster to send your ad out to numerous lower quality places.
9. **Test, Update and Modify**. Review, change and add to your PPC keywords. Submit more articles and adverts. Start tactfully promoting your products in the forums.

Your challenge will be to be listed in the major search engines and then get traffic. Now market your web site like mad.

It will take several months to make an impact in the major search engines. So build up your local custom whilst you are doing this. www.GetIntoGoogleFast.com – Does exactly what is says in the domain!

If you require business consultancy, or have comments on this book, please contact us on

sales@BizGuruServices.com or at

www.ProjectNiche.com

## Proposal Management and Bid Management

**Proposal Writing For Smaller Businesses *Who Want To Become Bigger Businesses:*** Are you a small or medium business who wants to grow bigger but you are not sure how to? Do you wish to bid or tender for business and not sure how to go about it? Do you keep writing proposals and never seem to win anything? Does your company wish to tender for extra work in order to expand? Then this book is for you. Written especially for the smaller business by an international bid manager who works with small and medium businesses this book explains everything your need to know to write a winning proposal in easy to understand terms. It includes preparing your company to write winning proposals, how to write and present your tender, understand risk and ask your client the correct questions. Loads of standard documents and lists to use, some great advice and warnings about what can go wrong – what more can you want?

**FastTrack© Bid Management:** From Wish To Win With The Bid Manager's Handbook! Bid Management THE skill that takes your company from Wish To Win! Learn how to improve your chances of winning that that proposal whilst minimising your risk and maximizing your profit. Learn the Bid Methodology SuperBid - to move you from Wish to Win in a logical and organized way. Understand how to identify and mitigate risks found lurking in those invitations to tender documents. Ensure that you produce a winning proposal that highlights your companies strengths and hides your weaknesses.

**FastTrack© The Winning Solution:** Do you wish to bid or tender for business and not sure how to go about it? Do you keep bidding and never seem to be considered? Does your company wish to tender for extra work in order to expand? This book will show you not only how to prepare your company, but also present your capabilities and strengths in the best possible manner. Preparing the proposed solution is always a problem for companies that do not normally undertake project management. This book provides the basics of project management and how to define the proposed solution to the tendering body. Risks are the greatest reason for failure to make a profit from your winning bid.

**FastTrack© Project Management:** Do you want to know what project management is all about or just want your company's projects to run more smoothly? Are all your projects being run in different ineffective ways? Do you want some in depth consistency in your project management? Or even worse, do you not know what is happening with the projects in your company? You need FastTrack Project Management – the Project Manager's Handbook. Learn how to plan a project and keep it on track! Control all the changes and problems as well as document them for later reference. Let all your team, users and clients understand what is going on and the successes that you have had. Identify the various project stages, staff and control methods as well as detailing the main project documentation used within a project. Understand how to manage a project effectively, efficiently and profitably. Understand project controls, documentation, planning, management and communication with our detailed methods and processes.

www.ingramcontent.com/pod-product-compliance
Lightning Source LLC
LaVergne TN
LVHW090948080826
845145LV00003B/928

* 9 7 8 0 9 5 6 3 8 6 1 4 4 *